I0087496

Knowledge Drops - Biology 1

Knowledge Drops Biology, Volume 1

Christobal Watson Hernandez

Published by Chipped Feather Productions, 2023.

KNOWLEDGE DROPS - BIOLOGY 1

First edition. June 3, 2023.

Copyright © 2023 Christobal Watson Hernandez.

ISBN: 978-0473680930

Written by Christobal Watson Hernandez.

Table of Contents

Knowledge Drops

Biology 1

"The more we know, the more we realize how much we have yet to discover."

- Cristóbal Watson Hernandez

CHRISTOBAL WATSON HERNANDEZ

KNOWLEDGE DROPS - BIOLOGY 1

Discover the captivating world of scientific biology through "Knowledge Drops," an engaging exploration of 50 thought-provoking questions and their enlightening answers.

In this accessible and captivating non-fiction book, Jonas Keep takes you on a journey into the depths of scientific biology, breaking down complex concepts into digestible nuggets of knowledge. Whether you're a curious student, a science enthusiast, or simply intrigued by the wonders of life, this book is your gateway to understanding the fundamental principles that shape our biological world.

"Knowledge Drops" goes beyond textbook explanations, offering accessible explanations and real-world examples that will ignite your curiosity.

Prepare to be amazed as you uncover the wonders of scientific biology, unlocking a world of understanding and appreciation for the intricate mechanisms that govern life on Earth. Let "Knowledge Drops" be your guide on this captivating journey of discovery.

Why do freshwater lakes & rivers seem to have less biological structure than oceans?

———

F reshwater lakes and rivers often appear to have fewer plants and animals compared to oceans because of a few important reasons.

Firstly, oceans receive more nutrients than freshwater systems. Nutrients are like food for plants and animals. In the ocean, there are many sources of nutrients, such as rivers that bring in nutrients from the land, and marine organisms that release nutrients when they die. These nutrients support the growth of tiny plants called phytoplankton, which are the foundation of the marine food chain. In freshwater, the amount of nutrients is usually lower, so there is less food available for plants and animals to grow and survive.

Secondly, the size and connections of oceans play a role. Oceans are vast and interconnected, allowing plants and animals to move around and find new places to live. This helps them find enough food and mates. It also allows for the exchange of genetic material, which leads to more diversity. In contrast, freshwater systems like lakes and rivers are often smaller and more isolated. They may not be connected to other bodies of water, which limits the movement of plants and animals. This means that the variety of species and interactions in freshwater systems can be less than in the ocean.

Finally, the stability of the environment is another factor. Oceans tend to have more stable conditions, such as constant water temperature and salinity. This stability allows marine organisms to adapt to specific habitats and develop specialized roles in the ecosystem. Freshwater systems can be more variable in their conditions, with changing water levels, temperatures, and other factors. This variability can make it more challenging for organisms to establish stable populations and complex relationships.

Overall, these factors contribute to the perception that freshwater lakes and rivers have less biological structure compared to oceans.

Did the beginning of the latest Ice Age cause widespread extinction?

———

Yes, the beginning of the latest Ice Age, known as the Pleistocene Epoch, did indeed cause the widespread extinction of various plant and animal species. During this period, which began approximately 2.6 million years ago and lasted until about 11,700 years ago, the Earth experienced a series of glacial and interglacial cycles, with alternating periods of colder and warmer temperatures.

The onset of the Ice Age led to significant changes in global climate and environment, including the expansion of ice sheets, the formation of glaciers, and changes in sea levels. These changes had a profound impact on ecosystems and the survival of many species.

The cooling temperatures and expanding ice sheets caused a decrease in available habitats and resources, which put pressure on numerous plants and animals. Many species that were adapted to warmer conditions and specialized environments struggled to survive in the harsher and more limited conditions of the Ice Age. Consequently, a significant number of species went extinct during this period.

Some of the well-known extinct species from the Pleistocene Epoch include the woolly mammoth, saber-toothed cats, giant ground sloths, and the Irish elk. These extinctions were likely a result of a combination of factors, including habitat loss, competition for resources, and the inability of some species to adapt to the changing climate.

It's important to note that while the Ice Age did cause widespread extinction, it also provided opportunities for new species to evolve and adapt to the changing environment. The fluctuating climate and the presence of different habitats during glacial and interglacial periods played a role in shaping the biodiversity we see today.

Why can't humans contract viruses from eating infected animals?

———

Humans cannot contract certain viruses by eating infected animals because viruses have a preference for specific species. Each virus is specialized to infect and reproduce within particular organisms or groups of organisms.

When a virus infects an animal, it interacts with specific parts of the animal's cells. However, the cells in humans are different from those in animals, making it difficult for the virus to enter and infect human cells.

Additionally, animals and humans have different immune systems that help fight off viruses. The immune systems of animals and humans work in slightly different ways, meaning that a virus adapted to an animal's immune system may not be able to effectively infect humans.

Furthermore, our digestive system plays a role. When we eat an infected animal, our digestive processes break down the animal's tissues and the viruses present in them. This process can weaken or destroy the viruses, reducing their ability to cause infection in our bodies.

Why do peacocks have such flamboyant feathers?

———

Peacocks have flamboyant feathers because they use them to attract a mate. In the bird world, males often have bright and showy features to catch the attention of females. The male peacock's colorful and elaborate feathers are like a fancy outfit or a beautiful costume they wear to impress the female peahens.

The feathers of a peacock are mostly displayed during courtship rituals. When a male peacock wants to attract a female, he spreads his long, colorful tail feathers into a big, eye-catching fan shape. He also shakes them and makes a special sound to get the female's attention. This display is like a special dance or performance to show off how attractive he is.

The bright colors and patterns of the peacock's feathers make the male stand out and look very special. The female peahens, who have more plain-looking feathers, are attracted to the male with the most vibrant and impressive feathers. They see his feathers as a sign that he is healthy, and strong, and would be a good partner to have chicks with.

So, the flamboyant feathers of peacocks serve a specific purpose in their natural world. They help the males attract a mate and show off their qualities to the females. It's like wearing a beautiful outfit or using fancy decorations to get someone's attention and impress them.

Why do gnats swarm in columns?

———

G nats swarm in columns for many reasons including because it helps them find food and stay safe. Gnats are very tiny insects that often gather together in large groups called swarms. These swarms can sometimes form a column shape, which means they line up on top of each other in a tall, narrow group.

One reason why gnats swarm in columns is for navigation. Gnats use visual cues to move around, and when they see other gnats flying in a column, they can follow the movement of the group. This helps them stay together and find their way to food sources, like flowers or decaying organic matter.

Another reason for swarming in columns is safety. In a column formation, the gnats can protect themselves from predators. By staying close together, they make it harder for predators, like birds, to catch and eat them. It's like forming a big group where it's harder for someone to single out and catch just one gnat.

Additionally, swarming in columns also helps with mating. When gnats are ready to reproduce, they gather in large swarms, including in column formations. This allows males and females to find each other more easily and mate.

So, the columns of gnats you see are actually their way of moving together, finding food, staying safe from predators, and even finding mates. It's a behavior they have developed to survive and thrive in their environment.

Prior to the discovery of yeast, how did people explain fermentation?

———

Before the discovery of yeast, people had different explanations for fermentation. Fermentation is a process that happens when certain foods or liquids change their properties, like when grape juice turns into wine or when dough rises to make bread.

One explanation that people had before knowing about yeast was called the "vital force" theory. They believed that there was a special life force or energy in certain substances that caused them to ferment. They thought this force made the changes happen, but they didn't understand exactly how it worked.

Another explanation was called the "chemical theory." Some people believed that fermentation was caused by a chemical reaction happening in the food or liquid. They thought that substances in the ingredients combined and changed, creating the fermentation process.

People also observed that fermentation often happened in warm and humid conditions. They noticed that if they left fruit juice or grains in a warm and moist environment, they would start to change and become fermented. So, they associated the process with environmental conditions rather than understanding the specific biological factors involved.

It was only later, in the mid-19th century, that scientists discovered yeast and its role in fermentation. They realized that tiny organisms, like yeast, were actually responsible for the fermentation process. These organisms eat the sugars in the food or liquid and produce alcohol and carbon dioxide as byproducts.

So, before the discovery of yeast, people had different ideas about fermentation. They thought it was caused by a mysterious life force, a chemical reaction, or environmental conditions. But it was through scientific advancements and research that the role of yeast in fermentation was eventually understood.

How do whales dive so deep and resurface without getting the bends?

———

Whales are able to dive deep and resurface without getting the bends because their bodies are adapted to handle the changes in pressure underwater. The bends, also known as decompression sickness, can happen when a person or animal ascends too quickly after being deep underwater for a long time.

When whales dive, they have a few special adaptations that help them avoid the bends. One important adaptation is their flexible ribcage. Unlike humans, whales can collapse their ribcage, which allows their lungs to compress as they go deeper. This helps to prevent damage to their lungs from the increasing pressure.

When a whale dives, it slows down its heart rate and reduces blood flow to non-essential areas. This helps to conserve oxygen and directs it to the most important organs, like the brain and heart. The whale's body also has a unique type of protein called myoglobin, which stores oxygen in the muscles and helps supply oxygen during long dives.

When it's time for the whale to come back to the surface, it gradually ascends at a controlled pace. This allows its body to adjust to the decreasing pressure and gives the dissolved gases, like nitrogen, time to safely leave its body without forming dangerous bubbles. By ascending slowly, the whale avoids the bends.

Do bats get mixed with each others echolocation signal?

E cholocation is a special ability that bats have to navigate and find their way in the dark. It works like a natural sonar system, similar to how submarines use sound waves to detect objects underwater.

Each bat emits its own unique echolocation signal. These signals are like little "clicks" or "chirps" that the bat makes. When the sound waves from the echolocation signal hit an object, they bounce back to the bat. By listening to the returning sound waves, the bat can figure out the distance, size, and shape of the object.

Even though many bats may be flying and using echolocation at the same time, they have the remarkable ability to distinguish their own echoes from the echoes of other bats. They do this by listening very carefully and paying attention to the timing and pattern of the returning sounds.

Bats can adjust the frequency and duration of their echolocation signals, which helps them avoid confusion. They can "tune in" to their own unique signals and filter out the signals from other bats. This way, they can focus on the information they need to navigate and find prey without getting mixed up with signals from other bats nearby.

So, bats have a remarkable ability to distinguish their own echolocation signals from those of other bats. They do this by listening carefully and adjusting their signals, which helps them navigate and hunt successfully in the dark without getting confused by signals from their fellow bats.

How is the distance an animal can smell calculated?

The distance an animal can smell is not typically calculated in a precise way like measuring a length with a ruler. Instead, scientists study and observe animals to understand their sense of smell and estimate the distance they can detect certain scents.

Animals have a much stronger sense of smell than humans. They have special receptors in their noses that can detect and analyze different smells in the environment. This sense of smell helps them find food, locate mates, identify predators, and navigate their surroundings.

To estimate the distance an animal can smell, scientists consider several factors. One important factor is the size and sensitivity of an animal's olfactory system, which includes its nose and brain. Animals with a larger and more developed olfactory system usually have a stronger sense of smell and can detect scents from greater distances.

Another factor is the scent's strength and environmental conditions. Some scents can travel far in the air, especially if there is no wind or if the air is humid. Strong scents, such as those from a predator or potential food source, are more likely to be detected from a greater distance.

Scientists also study the behavior of animals and their reactions to different scents. By observing how an animal responds to a scent or tracks it, scientists can make educated estimations about the distance from which the animal detected the scent.

It's important to note that the distance an animal can smell can vary greatly depending on the species, the environment, and the specific scent in question. Some animals, like bloodhounds or certain types of sharks, are known for their exceptional sense of smell and can detect scents from several kilometers away. Other animals may have a more limited range of smell.

How do invasive species manage to reproduce without severe inbreeding problems?

———

Invasive species can reproduce without severe inbreeding problems because they have different ways to maintain genetic diversity within their populations.

When a species becomes invasive in a new environment, it starts with a small number of individuals. This small population may have limited genetic diversity, which means they are closely related to each other. Inbreeding, which is mating between close relatives, can lead to problems such as reduced fertility and weaker offspring.

However, invasive species have strategies to overcome these problems. One way is that they often produce a large number of offspring. This is called high reproductive capacity. By having many offspring, there is more variation in the population. This helps to reduce the negative effects of inbreeding and increases the chances of having genetically diverse individuals.

Another strategy is that invasive species can quickly spread and establish new populations in different areas. This is known as rapid colonization. As these populations expand and interact with each other, they can exchange genetic material. This mixing of genes increases genetic diversity and reduces the risks associated with inbreeding.

Invasive species may also have adaptations that promote outcrossing. Outcrossing means that they mate with individuals from other populations rather than with close relatives. By mating with individuals from different populations, invasive species can introduce new genes into their population and maintain genetic diversity.

Furthermore, some invasive species have mechanisms to prevent self-fertilization or have ways to recognize and avoid mating with close relatives. These mechanisms help to ensure that individuals mate with genetically different partners, which reduces the likelihood of inbreeding.

However, it's important to remember that while invasive species can avoid severe inbreeding problems, they can still have negative impacts on ecosystems and native species. Their ability to reproduce rapidly and outcompete native species can disrupt the balance of ecosystems and threaten biodiversity.

Why have box jellyfish evolved to be so venomous?

———

B ox jellyfish have evolved to be venomous because it helps them survive and catch their prey. Their venom is a special adaptation that gives them an advantage in their environment.

The venom of box jellyfish serves two main purposes. First, it helps them immobilize and paralyze their prey. When a box jellyfish comes into contact with its prey, such as small fish or shrimp, it releases venom into the prey's body. This venom quickly immobilizes the prey, making it easier for the box jellyfish to catch and eat it.

Second, the venom of box jellyfish acts as a defense mechanism. If a predator or other threat comes into contact with their tentacles, the venom can deter or injure the attacker. This helps protect the box jellyfish from being eaten or harmed by other animals.

Over time, box jellyfish have evolved to produce more potent venom to increase their chances of catching prey and defending themselves effectively. This adaptation has allowed them to survive and thrive in their marine habitats.

It is important to note that while box jellyfish venom is dangerous to their prey and potential threats, it can also be harmful to humans. Their stings can cause painful reactions and, in rare cases, more severe effects. It's essential to exercise caution and follow safety guidelines when swimming or snorkeling in areas where box jellyfish are present.

Do animals observe or respond to the Aurora Borealis?

———

The evidence of animals observing or responding to the aurora borealis, also known as the Northern Lights, is limited. While there are some observations and anecdotes suggesting that certain animals may react to the aurora borealis, scientific research on this topic is relatively scarce.

Animals rely on their senses to navigate their surroundings and respond to various stimuli. However, their sensitivity and response to the aurora borealis, which is a natural light display in the sky, have not been extensively studied.

Some reports suggest that certain animals, such as reindeer and sled dogs, may react to the aurora borealis. For example, it has been suggested that reindeer might exhibit behavioral changes or movement patterns when the lights are present. However, these observations are largely based on traditional knowledge and folklore rather than scientific studies.

One reason for the limited research on this topic is the challenging nature of studying animal responses to the aurora borealis. The phenomenon is often seen in remote and inhospitable regions, making it difficult to conduct controlled experiments or directly observe animals in their natural habitats.

Furthermore, animals may have different visual capabilities and sensitivities to light compared to humans, which could affect their perception and response to the aurora borealis. More research is needed to understand the specific ways in which animals might observe or respond to this natural phenomenon.

How do animals that can change colors to match surroundings know the color?

―――

A nimals that can change colors to match their surroundings, like chameleons or certain types of octopuses, have a special ability called camouflage. They change their color to blend in with their environment, which helps them hide from predators or sneak up on prey.

These animals have specialized cells in their skin called chromatophores. Chromatophores contain pigments, which are substances that give color to their skin. These pigments can expand or contract, causing changes in the animal's coloration.

Now, how do these animals know which color to change to? It's not that they see the color directly like we do. Instead, they use other cues in their environment to determine what color to become.

For example, if a chameleon wants to blend in with a green leaf, it might look at the surroundings and notice the green color of the leaf. The chameleon's brain processes this information and sends signals to the chromatophores in its skin. The chromatophores then adjust their pigments to match the color of the leaf.

Similarly, octopuses have special cells in their skin called iridophores and leucophores that can change their color and reflect light differently. They use light receptors in their skin to identify the colors and patterns around them. The information is processed by their brain, and signals are sent to the iridophores and leucophores to adjust their coloration accordingly.

It's important to note that these color-changing abilities are not conscious decisions made by the animals. They have evolved over time to help them survive in their environments. The animals' bodies have developed mechanisms to detect and respond to certain visual cues in their surroundings, triggering changes in their skin color.

Can wildlife genetic diversity be increased with cloning?

———

C loning is a scientific process that involves creating an exact genetic copy, or clone, of an organism. While cloning can replicate the genetic material of a specific individual, it does not necessarily increase the overall genetic diversity of a wildlife population.

Genetic diversity refers to the variety of different genes within a population. It is important for the long-term survival and adaptability of species because it allows them to better respond to changes in their environment, resist diseases, and maintain overall population health.

Cloning involves taking genetic material, such as DNA, from a single individual and creating an identical copy. This means that the genetic diversity of the cloned individual is exactly the same as the original organism. In other words, cloning does not introduce any new genetic variation.

To increase genetic diversity, it is essential to have a mixture of different genes from a broader population. This is typically achieved through natural reproduction, where individuals with different genetic traits come together to produce offspring.

CHRISTOBAL WATSON HERNANDEZ

While cloning can be useful in certain situations, such as preserving endangered species or producing specific individuals for scientific research, it is not an effective method for increasing genetic diversity on a larger scale. To ensure healthy and diverse wildlife populations, it is crucial to focus on protecting natural habitats, preserving ecosystems, and maintaining healthy populations of animals that can naturally reproduce and pass on their unique genetic traits to future generations.

Do animals have a wide range of different sicknesses like humans do?

A nimals, like humans, can experience a wide range of different sicknesses, although the specific types of illnesses may vary between species. Just like humans, animals can get sick from infections, diseases, and other health conditions.

Animals can suffer from various types of illnesses, including bacterial infections, viral infections, parasitic infestations, and diseases caused by environmental factors. These illnesses can affect different parts of an animal's body, such as its respiratory system, digestive system, skin, or internal organs.

Just like humans, animals have immune systems that help protect them against diseases. However, different species of animals have varying levels of susceptibility to certain illnesses. Some diseases may affect multiple species, while others may be specific to certain types of animals.

Animals in the wild can encounter health challenges from factors like exposure to parasites, changes in their natural habitats, or interactions with other animals carrying diseases. Domesticated animals, such as pets or livestock, may face additional risks due to close contact with humans, interactions with other animals, or living conditions that can promote the spread of diseases.

It's important to note that animals and humans can sometimes transmit diseases to each other. These are known as zoonotic diseases. Examples include rabies, certain types of influenza, and certain parasitic infections. It highlights the importance of proper hygiene and precautions when interacting with animals, especially if they are wild or have an unknown health history.

Do germs move around on a hard surface?

―――

Germs, which are tiny microorganisms like bacteria or viruses, can move around on hard surfaces, but they don't move by themselves like animals do. Instead, they can be transferred from one surface to another through various means.

When people or animals touch a contaminated surface, such as a doorknob or a table, germs can stick to their hands or paws. If they then touch another surface, they can leave behind some of the germs on that new surface. This is how germs can spread from one place to another.

Germs can also be transferred through other means, such as sneezing or coughing. When someone sneezes or coughs, tiny droplets containing germs can be released into the air. If these droplets land on a hard surface, the germs can stay there and potentially infect someone else who touches that surface.

It's important to note that not all germs are the same, and some can survive longer on surfaces than others. Some germs can only survive for a short time outside of a host (a person or an animal), while others can survive for longer periods. The length of time a germ can survive on a surface depends on various factors such as temperature, humidity, and the specific type of germ.

To help prevent the spread of germs, it's important to practice good hygiene. This includes washing hands regularly with soap and water, especially after touching surfaces that may be contaminated. Using hand sanitizers can also help kill germs on the hands when soap and water are not available. Cleaning and disinfecting frequently touched surfaces, such as doorknobs, light switches, and countertops, can also help reduce the number of germs present.

What makes a seed start to grow when it is planted?

―――

S eeds are amazing little packages that have the ability to remain dormant, or inactive, for a long time until they are planted. When the right conditions are met, a seed starts to grow and develop into a new plant. So, what triggers a seed to start growing?

Seeds need specific environmental conditions to begin their growth process. The main factors that influence seed germination, which is the process of a seed sprouting and developing into a plant, are water, temperature, and sometimes light.

Firstly, when a seed is planted in soil, it needs water to become hydrated. Water helps to soften the outer coat of the seed, allowing it to absorb nutrients and swell. This hydration process activates the biochemical reactions within the seed that initiate growth.

Secondly, temperature plays an important role. Different plants have different temperature preferences for germination. Some seeds prefer warmer temperatures, while others prefer cooler temperatures. When the seed senses the right temperature, it triggers the activation of enzymes, which are substances that help break down stored nutrients within the seed. These nutrients provide the energy and building blocks for the new plant to grow.

Lastly, light can also be a factor for certain seeds, although not all seeds require light to germinate. Some seeds, like those from many flowering plants, need exposure to light to start growing. On the other hand, some seeds prefer darkness and will only sprout if covered by soil.

Once the seed has absorbed water, the temperature is suitable, and the light conditions (if needed) are met, the seed will start to germinate. It sends out a tiny root, known as a radicle, which anchors the plant into the soil. Then, a shoot emerges above the soil, containing the stem and leaves of the new plant. From there, the plant continues to grow and develop, utilizing the stored nutrients within the seed.

How many species of mammal survived the asteroid impact?

─────

When a large asteroid collided with Earth millions of years ago, it caused a major event known as the "asteroid impact." This event had a significant impact on many living organisms, including mammals. While the asteroid impact caused widespread extinction, some mammal species managed to survive. However, it's important to note that the exact number of surviving mammal species is uncertain, as it happened a long time ago and evidence can be limited.

The asteroid impact led to drastic changes in the environment, including widespread fires, tsunamis, and a release of dust and debris into the atmosphere. These changes affected many species, causing them to die out. However, some mammals were able to survive because they had certain adaptations or lived in environments that provided them with better chances of survival.

Some theories suggest that smaller mammals, like small rodents or insect-eating creatures, were more likely to survive the asteroid impact. These animals may have found shelter in burrows or small spaces, allowing them to escape some of the immediate dangers. Additionally, mammals that lived in aquatic environments, such as dolphins or whales, were also more likely to survive because the impact's effects were less severe underwater.

CHRISTOBAL WATSON HERNANDEZ

It's important to remember that the asteroid impact resulted in a mass extinction event, meaning that a large number of species, including many mammals, became extinct. However, some mammal species managed to survive and eventually diversified, leading to the wide variety of mammals we have today.

Scientists have discovered fossil records and conducted research to better understand the effects of the asteroid's impact on mammal populations. These studies provide valuable insights into the survival and evolution of mammals during that time. By examining these fossils and studying the genetic relationships of living species, scientists can gain a better understanding of which mammals managed to survive and how they adapted to the changing environment.

How do self-pollinating plants get enough genetic diversity to not be damaged by inbreeding?

———

Self-pollinating plants have a clever way of ensuring they have enough genetic diversity to avoid the negative effects of inbreeding. Inbreeding happens when closely related individuals mate and pass on similar genes to their offspring, which can lead to problems.

To prevent inbreeding, self-pollinating plants have developed mechanisms that introduce some genetic diversity. While they can pollinate themselves, they also have ways to receive pollen from other plants, which helps in mixing up their genes.

One way self-pollinating plants achieve this is through a process called "self-incompatibility." It means that even though they can produce pollen, their own pollen is unable to fertilize their own eggs. Instead, the plant's flowers have certain structures that prevent self-fertilization. This forces the plant to receive pollen from other plants, either through wind, insects, or other means.

By receiving pollen from other plants, self-pollinating plants introduce new genetic material. This genetic exchange helps maintain diversity in their offspring and reduces the negative effects of inbreeding. It's like adding a little bit of variation to their genetic pool.

Another way self-pollinating plants ensure genetic diversity is through occasional mutations. Mutations are changes in the genetic material of an organism that can happen randomly. These mutations can introduce new traits and characteristics in the plant population, adding to their genetic diversity.

While self-pollinating plants have mechanisms to increase genetic diversity, it's important to note that they generally have lower genetic diversity compared to plants that rely on cross-pollination with other individuals. This is because self-pollinating plants primarily reproduce with themselves, which limits the introduction of new genetic material.

However, even with lower genetic diversity, self-pollinating plants have evolved ways to ensure their survival and adapt to their environment. They have traits and adaptations that allow them to thrive in specific conditions, and their ability to self-pollinate provides a reliable way to reproduce even when other pollinators are scarce.

Has life emerged multiple times on Earth?

———

The question of whether life has emerged multiple times on Earth is still a topic of scientific investigation and debate. While there is no definitive evidence yet, scientists have discovered some interesting clues that suggest the possibility of life emerging more than once on our planet.

The idea that life may have emerged multiple times is based on the discovery of organisms called extremophiles. Extremophiles are living things that can survive and thrive in extreme environments, such as deep-sea hydrothermal vents, acidic lakes, or hot springs. These environments were once thought to be inhospitable for life.

The presence of extremophiles suggests that life may have originated and adapted to different environments independently. It's like having different groups of organisms that evolved separately to survive in their unique habitats.

Another clue comes from the study of ancient fossils. Scientists have found microfossils, which are tiny preserved remains of ancient life, that date back billions of years. These microfossils provide evidence that life existed on Earth long ago. Some scientists propose that these ancient life forms could be the remnants of separate origin events, indicating the possibility of multiple emergences of life.

However, it's important to note that the question of multiple emergences of life on Earth is challenging to answer definitively. The study of life's origins is a complex field, and scientists continue to explore and gather more evidence to better understand this fascinating topic.

Why do humans and birds share so many diseases?

―――――

Humans and birds share some diseases because certain viruses and bacteria can infect both species. There are a few reasons why this happens.

Some diseases are caused by microorganisms like viruses or bacteria, which can infect different species of animals, including humans and birds. When these microorganisms find a suitable host, they can cause infections and make the host sick.

Birds and humans often live in close proximity to each other. Humans have domesticated certain bird species, such as chickens and ducks, for various purposes like food production or companionship. This close contact increases the chances of disease transmission between humans and birds.

Some diseases can be transmitted between species through vectors. Vectors are organisms, like mosquitoes or ticks, that can carry disease-causing microorganisms from one host to another. For example, mosquitoes can carry viruses that cause diseases like dengue fever or West Nile virus, which can infect both humans and birds.

The genetic similarity between humans and birds can also play a role. Birds and humans share some genetic similarities, especially in the basic structure and functioning of their cells. This similarity can sometimes make it easier for certain diseases to cross over between the two species.

To prevent the spread of diseases between humans and birds, it's important to practice good hygiene and take necessary precautions. For example, maintaining cleanliness in areas where birds are kept, washing hands thoroughly after handling birds or their droppings, and avoiding direct contact with sick birds can help reduce the risk of disease transmission.

Why are some people more appealing to mosquitoes than others?

———

Mosquitoes have a tendency to be more attracted to certain individuals than others. There are several factors that contribute to this preference.

One factor is body odor. Mosquitoes are drawn to the scents and chemicals that our bodies produce, particularly those emitted through sweat. Each person has a unique scent based on their genetic makeup, diet, and the bacteria on their skin. Some people naturally produce more chemicals that are appealing to mosquitoes, making them more attractive targets for mosquito bites.

Another factor is body heat. Mosquitoes are sensitive to heat and can detect the warmth given off by our bodies. Some individuals may have slightly higher body temperatures or generate more heat, which can make them more noticeable to mosquitoes.

Furthermore, mosquitoes are attracted to carbon dioxide, a gas that we exhale when we breathe. People who exhale more carbon dioxide may be more attractive to mosquitoes. Factors that can influence carbon dioxide production include physical activity, metabolic rate, and even pregnancy.

It's important to note that genetics and individual variations play a significant role in attracting mosquitoes. While certain traits may make someone more appealing to mosquitoes, it doesn't mean they are more susceptible to diseases transmitted by mosquitoes. Mosquitoes are opportunistic feeders and may bite anyone in their quest for a blood meal.

How do ant colonies circulate air?

———

Inside ant nests, there are tunnels and chambers that ants build. These tunnels connect different parts of the nest and create pathways for air to flow. Some tunnels even reach the surface of the ground or connect to cracks in tree trunks, allowing fresh air to enter.

Ants help circulate the air by moving around inside the tunnels. As they move, they create air currents that push the air through the nest. This movement helps to bring in fresh oxygen and remove stale air.

When ants move inside the tunnels, they also create space for air to flow. As they crawl through the chambers, the air gets pushed along and reaches different areas of the nest. This movement of ants helps to distribute the air evenly.

In this way, ant colonies ensure that there is a constant supply of fresh air circulating within their nests. It allows the ants to breathe in oxygen and expel carbon dioxide, which keeps the air quality suitable for their survival.

Why do city pigeons so often have mutilated feet?

Y̶ou may have noticed that pigeons in cities sometimes have mutilated or injured feet. There are a few reasons why this happens.

City environments can be challenging for pigeons. The concrete and hard surfaces in urban areas are not natural habitats for them. Pigeons' feet are adapted for perching on branches and natural surfaces, not for walking or landing on hard concrete. When they constantly walk or land on rough surfaces like pavement or rooftops, it can cause wear and tear on their feet, leading to injuries and deformities.

Pigeons also often scavenge for food in urban areas. They might search for food scraps on the ground or rummage through garbage bins. Unfortunately, city streets can be littered with sharp objects like broken glass, nails, or other debris that can injure their feet when they walk or land on them.

Another factor is the presence of predators. Cities are home to many predators, such as cats and birds of prey, that pose a threat to pigeons. To protect themselves, pigeons may need to quickly take off or fly away, sometimes causing them to land awkwardly or abruptly, which can lead to foot injuries.

It's also worth noting that some cases of mutilated feet in city pigeons may be caused by diseases or infections. Pigeons in urban environments often gather in large numbers, which can facilitate the spread of diseases and parasites that affect their feet.

Can we selectively breed cows to produce less methane?

———

Yes, we can selectively breed cows to produce less methane. Methane is a gas that cows naturally release during digestion, and it contributes to global warming. Through a process called selective breeding, we can choose cows with certain traits and characteristics that produce less methane.

Selective breeding is a way of carefully choosing which cows will be the parents of the next generation. By selecting cows with lower methane emissions and breeding them together, we can increase the likelihood that their offspring will also have reduced methane production.

Scientists and farmers can use various methods to identify cows with lower methane emissions. They may measure the amount of methane produced by individual cows using special equipment or monitor other traits related to methane production, such as feed efficiency or the composition of microbes in their digestive system.

Over time, by consistently breeding cows with lower methane emissions, we can create a population of cows that are more environmentally friendly and produce less methane.

It's important to note that selective breeding is just one of the approaches used to address methane emissions from cows. Other strategies include improving their diet, developing new feeding techniques, and exploring alternative feed additives that can reduce methane production.

Why are seashells shaped the way they are?

———

Seashells come in many different shapes, sizes, and patterns, and they serve important purposes for the animals that live inside them. The shape of a seashell is influenced by several factors.

The shape of a seashell helps protect the animal that lives inside. The hard outer layer of the shell provides a strong barrier against predators and harsh environmental conditions. The shape can also help the animal blend in with its surroundings, making it less visible to predators.

the shape of a seashell is influenced by the animal's body structure and its needs for survival. Different types of animals have different body shapes and lifestyles. Some animals have long, spiral-shaped shells, while others have flat or rounded shells. These shapes provide the right amount of space and support for the animal's body to fit inside and allow for movement.

Another factor that affects seashell shape is the environment in which the animal lives. Seashells are often shaped by the currents and waves of the ocean. Strong currents can cause shells to have streamlined shapes, allowing them to move through the water more easily. In contrast, shells found in calmer waters may have more delicate and intricate shapes.

Additionally, the shape of a seashell can also help with buoyancy. Some shells are designed to help the animal float or stay balanced in the water. This is particularly important for animals that live near the surface or need to move between different depths.

Why does alcohol kill all germs?

———

Alcohol is known for its ability to kill germs, including bacteria. When we use alcohol-based hand sanitizers or disinfectants, they work by destroying the germs on our hands or surfaces. However, not all germs are equally affected by alcohol, and there are some extremophile bacteria that can tolerate or survive in alcohol.

Alcohol kills germs by disrupting their cellular structure and functions. When alcohol comes into contact with bacteria, it can penetrate their outer protective layers, such as the cell membrane. Once inside the bacterial cell, alcohol can interfere with important cellular processes, such as protein and enzyme function. This disruption ultimately leads to the death of the bacteria.

However, it's important to note that while alcohol is effective against many types of bacteria, there are some extremophile bacteria that have adapted to survive in extreme environments, including high concentrations of alcohol. These bacteria have developed special mechanisms to protect themselves from the harmful effects of alcohol. They may have thicker cell walls or other protective features that make them more resistant.

In general, though, alcohol is a reliable germ-killing agent and widely used for disinfection purposes. It's important to use alcohol-based products properly and follow the recommended guidelines for effective germ control.

Why were some terrestrial dinosaurs so much larger than current animals?

———

Some terrestrial dinosaurs were much larger than current animals for a few reasons. One main reason is that dinosaurs lived in a different time period called the Mesozoic Era, which was millions of years ago. During this time, the environment was different, providing favorable conditions for dinosaurs to grow to enormous sizes.

Dinosaurs had fewer natural predators compared to animals today. This allowed them to grow larger without the constant threat of being hunted. With fewer predators to worry about, they could allocate more energy and resources toward growth and survival.

The availability of food played a significant role. Dinosaurs lived during a time when the Earth had abundant plant life. This provided a vast food supply for herbivorous dinosaurs, allowing them to eat and grow larger. Carnivorous dinosaurs, in turn, had plenty of herbivorous dinosaurs to prey upon, ensuring a sufficient food source for their own growth.

Additionally, dinosaurs had different body structures that allowed for large size. They had strong and sturdy bones to support their weight, and some species had long necks and tails to balance their bodies. These adaptations helped them move and survive as larger creatures.

Over time, through a process called evolution, certain dinosaur species developed characteristics that favored larger body sizes. These adaptations allowed them to thrive and dominate their ecosystems. However, it's important to note that not all dinosaurs were enormous. There were also smaller dinosaur species that occupied different ecological niches.

How did eye lenses evolve?

The evolution of eye lenses is an interesting process that took place over millions of years. It involved gradual changes and adaptations in the eyes of different organisms.

In the earliest forms of life, there were no eyes as we know them today. However, some simple organisms could sense light using light-sensitive cells. These cells could detect changes in light intensity but did not form images.

Over time, some organisms developed a depression in their light-sensitive cells, creating a small pit. This pit helped them sense the direction of light more accurately. This pit was like a primitive eye, but it couldn't form clear images yet.

As evolution continued, the pit gradually deepened and formed a cup-like structure. This structure allowed the organism to detect the direction of light more precisely. Eventually, a transparent layer covered the top of the cup, forming a basic lens. The lens helped focus light onto the light-sensitive cells, allowing for clearer vision.

As organisms with these cup-like eyes evolved further, the lenses became more complex. They became thicker and more curved, which improved their ability to focus light. This advancement led to the formation of a clear image on the light-sensitive cells at the back of the eye.

In more advanced organisms, such as fish, reptiles, birds, and mammals, the lens continued to evolve. It became more flexible, allowing for better focusing on objects at different distances. This flexibility allowed these organisms to see objects both near and far more clearly.

The evolution of eye lenses involved small changes and adaptations over long periods of time. Each change provided a slight advantage, which increased the chances of survival and reproduction for the organisms that possessed them. Through this gradual process of natural selection, more complex and sophisticated eye lenses evolved.

Today, we see a wide variety of eye lenses across different species, each suited to their specific needs and environments.

Do butterflies have any memory of being a caterpillar?

———

B utterflies go through a remarkable transformation during their life cycle, starting as caterpillars and then turning into butterflies. While butterflies don't have the same kind of memory as humans, they do retain certain information and experiences from their time as caterpillars.

When a caterpillar undergoes metamorphosis and transforms into a butterfly, it goes through a dramatic physiological and behavioral change. During this process, the caterpillar's body breaks down, and a completely new body structure, including wings, forms inside the pupa. Once the butterfly emerges, it is indeed a new animal in terms of its physical appearance and abilities.

While the butterfly's memories from its caterpillar stage are not the same as human memories, some studies suggest that butterflies can retain certain information. For example, they can remember experiences related to feeding, mating, and avoiding predators. This information is likely stored in their nervous system.

Additionally, butterflies have instinctual behaviors that are crucial for their survival. These behaviors, such as finding nectar, choosing suitable host plants for laying eggs, and migrating long distances, are often guided by genetic programming rather than individual memory.

It's important to note that the lifespan of a butterfly is relatively short, usually just a few weeks or even days. This limited lifespan means that they don't have a long time to accumulate and retain memories as humans do. However, their instincts and genetic programming play a significant role in guiding their behaviors and ensuring their survival.

Do most animals have to worry about complications from cannibalization?

———

C annibalization, which means one animal eating another animal of the same species, is not very common in most animal populations. In general, animals tend to avoid cannibalizing their own kind. However, there are some instances where cannibalism can occur, and it may have certain implications or complications for the animals involved.

Cannibalism is more likely to happen in certain situations. For example, when there is a scarcity of food or when an animal is very hungry, it may resort to cannibalism as a way to survive. This can sometimes occur among certain species of insects, spiders, or even some fish. However, it's important to note that cannibalism is not a common behavior across most animal species.

In terms of complications, cannibalization can have negative effects on the population and individuals involved. Eating a member of the same species can lead to a loss of genetic diversity within the population. This is because individuals with certain genetic traits are being removed, which may reduce the overall genetic variability and adaptation potential of the species.

Additionally, cannibalism can transmit diseases or parasites between individuals. If an animal that is being eaten is infected with a disease or parasite, the cannibalistic predator may also become infected. This can potentially harm the health and survival of the cannibalistic individual.

Is there a quantifiable benefit to cooking food?

———

Cooking food offers several important benefits that can be measured and observed. One significant advantage is that cooking enhances the nutritional value of food. When we cook certain foods, like vegetables or grains, the heat breaks down their tough fibers and makes them easier to digest. This allows our bodies to absorb more nutrients, such as vitamins and minerals, which are essential for our health and well-being.

Furthermore, cooking plays a crucial role in food safety. By applying heat during the cooking process, harmful bacteria, parasites, and other microorganisms that may be present in raw food can be destroyed or reduced in number. This helps prevent food-borne illnesses and ensures that the food we eat is safer for consumption.

Another benefit of cooking is the improvement in taste and texture. Through cooking techniques like roasting, grilling, or frying, the flavors, aromas, and textures of food can be enhanced, making it more enjoyable to eat. This can stimulate our appetite and encourage us to consume a diverse range of nutritious foods.

Additionally, cooking makes food more digestible. The heat from cooking breaks down complex carbohydrates, proteins, and fats, making them easier for our bodies to break down and absorb. This promotes efficient digestion and allows us to extract energy from our food more effectively.

Can Viruses Transfer DNA segments from one species to another?

———

Viruses are tiny infectious agents that can infect cells and replicate inside them. They have genetic material, either DNA or RNA, that carries their instructions for making new copies of themselves. When a virus infects a cell, it injects its genetic material into the cell's own genetic material.

Sometimes, during this process, the viral genetic material can become integrated into the DNA of the infected cell. This means that the viral DNA becomes a part of the cell's genetic material. When the infected cell divides and reproduces, the viral DNA is also passed on to the new cells.

If the infected cell belongs to one species and gets infected by a virus from a different species, the viral DNA can carry genetic information from the original species to the new species. In this way, the virus acts as a carrier, transferring genetic material from one species to another.

This horizontal gene transfer can have important implications for the evolution of species. It can introduce new genes or genetic variations into a species, which can potentially lead to the development of new traits or adaptations. It can also contribute to the genetic diversity of populations.

Horizontal gene transfer facilitated by viruses is not the same as the normal way genetic information is passed down from parents to off-spring, which is called vertical gene transfer. Instead, it allows genetic material to move horizontally across different species boundaries.

How different were the first horses domesticated by humans compared to modern horses?

T he first horses that were domesticated by humans were smaller in size compared to the horses we see today. They were similar in size to ponies or small horses. Over time, through selective breeding, humans selectively chose larger horses for specific purposes like riding, pulling carts, or carrying heavy loads. This resulted in the development of larger horse breeds that we commonly see today.

Another difference is in their physical characteristics. The early domesticated horses had a different body shape compared to modern horses. They had shorter legs and a more compact body. Over many generations, humans selectively bred horses with longer legs and a leaner body structure, making them more suitable for tasks such as running, jumping, and carrying riders.

Furthermore, the first domesticated horses had different coat colors and patterns. They had a wider range of coat colors and patterns compared to modern horses. Through selective breeding, humans favored certain coat colors and patterns, leading to the development of specific horse breeds with distinct coat colors, such as solid black, chestnut, or spotted patterns like Appaloosa.

Lastly, the early domesticated horses had a different temperament compared to modern horses. They were less tolerant of human presence and had more instinctive and wild behavior. However, through generations of selective breeding and training, humans were able to develop calmer and more trainable horse breeds that are better suited for various activities like riding, racing, or working in agriculture.

How can a scientist tell the difference between blood samples from different animals?

———

S cientists can tell the difference between blood samples from different animals by studying certain characteristics and properties of the blood.

One way scientists can differentiate blood samples is by looking at the size and shape of the blood cells. Different animals have blood cells that vary in size and shape. For example, humans have round-shaped red blood cells, while other animals like dogs or cats may have oval-shaped or differently-sized blood cells. By examining these characteristics under a microscope, scientists can identify the species the blood sample belongs to.

Another important factor scientists consider is the presence of specific proteins or markers in the blood. Proteins are molecules found in the blood that perform various functions in the body. Different animals have different types and amounts of proteins in their blood. Scientists can use techniques like protein analysis or genetic testing to identify specific proteins or genetic markers that are unique to certain animal species. This helps them distinguish between blood samples from different animals.

Additionally, scientists can examine the DNA in the blood samples. DNA is the genetic material that carries the instructions for how living organisms develop and function. Each species has a unique DNA sequence. By comparing the DNA sequences from the blood samples, scientists can determine if they come from the same species or different species.

Furthermore, scientists may also consider other factors such as the presence of certain chemicals or substances in the blood that are specific to certain animals. These substances can include hormones, enzymes, or other biological molecules that are characteristic of particular species.

Are there any animals that need more than 2 parents to reproduce?

———

Most animals reproduce with the help of two parents, one male, and one female. However, there are a few exceptional cases where more than two parents are involved in the reproductive process.

One unique animal that requires more than two parents to reproduce is the honeybee. In a honeybee colony, there are three types of individuals: the queen, drones, and worker bees. When it comes to reproduction, the queen bee mates with multiple drones. Each drone contributes its genetic material to the queen during mating. The queen stores the collected sperm in her body for later use.

Once the queen has collected enough sperm, she uses it to fertilize her eggs. The fertilized eggs develop into female worker bees, which are responsible for tasks like collecting nectar, making honey, and taking care of the colony. The unfertilized eggs, on the other hand, develop into male drones. The drones' primary purpose is to mate with other queen bees from different colonies.

In this way, the honeybee colony requires genetic material from multiple drones, making it a cooperative effort involving more than two parents for successful reproduction.

It's important to note that while honeybees are an example of animals with more than two parents, they are relatively unique in this aspect. The vast majority of animal species reproduce with just two parents, one male, and one female.

What is the fastest-moving microorganism on the planet?

———

The fastest-moving microorganism on the planet is a type of bacterium called Vibrio alginolyticus. This bacterium lives in marine environments, such as the ocean. It has a long, whip-like structure called a flagellum that helps it move. The flagellum acts like a propeller, allowing the bacterium to swim through the water.

Vibrio alginolyticus can move very quickly. Scientists have measured its speed to be around 60 body lengths per second. That means if you were to compare it to a human, it would be like swimming at an incredible speed of about 500 kilometers per hour!

This high speed helps Vibrio alginolyticus to move around its environment effectively. It allows the bacterium to find food, avoid predators, and locate suitable places to live. With its fast swimming ability, Vibrio alginolyticus is able to navigate through water with great agility.

Do all animals regenerate their liver?

————

N ot all animals have the ability to regenerate their liver, but some animals do.

Regeneration is the process of growing back or repairing damaged or lost body parts. When it comes to the liver, some animals have the remarkable ability to regenerate it, which means they can grow a new liver if it gets damaged or removed.

Among the animals that can regenerate their liver are certain types of fish, such as the zebrafish, and certain reptiles, like the green anole lizard. These animals have the ability to regrow a fully functional liver, even if a large part of it is damaged or removed.

However, not all animals can regenerate their liver like these examples. Mammals, including humans, have limited regenerative abilities when it comes to the liver. While the liver can repair itself to some extent, it cannot fully regenerate a lost or severely damaged portion like fish or reptiles can.

Can spiders walk backward?

———

S piders are fascinating creatures with unique abilities, and one of them is their ability to walk backward. Just like humans and many other animals, spiders have legs that allow them to move in different directions, including backward.

Spiders have special joints in their legs that allow them to bend and move in various ways. These flexible joints give them the freedom to walk forward, sideways, and even backward. When a spider wants to move backward, it simply uses its leg muscles to push itself in the opposite direction.

Walking backward can be useful for spiders in certain situations. For example, if they need to retreat from a potential threat or navigate through tight spaces, walking backward allows them to move effectively and avoid obstacles in their path.

Why does temperature determine the sex of certain egg-laying animals?

———

Certain egg-laying animals, such as crocodiles, have a unique way of determining the sex of their offspring, and temperature plays a significant role in this process.

In animals like crocodiles, the sex of the offspring is not determined by genetics like in humans or many other animals. Instead, it is influenced by the temperature at which the eggs are incubated. This means that the temperature can determine whether a crocodile will be a male or a female.

When a female crocodile lays her eggs, she buries them in a nest or mound and carefully controls the conditions around the eggs. The temperature at which the eggs are kept during incubation is crucial in determining the sex of the developing crocodile.

Typically, higher temperatures during incubation tend to result in more male crocodiles, while lower temperatures result in more females. This is known as temperature-dependent sex determination (TSD). The exact temperature thresholds can vary among different species of crocodiles.

Scientists believe that specific temperature ranges influence the development of certain reproductive hormones in the embryos. These hormones, in turn, affect the sexual differentiation of the crocodile. It's like a "switch" that is triggered by the temperature, determining whether the embryo will develop as a male or a female.

This temperature-dependent sex determination is an interesting and unique characteristic of some egg-laying animals, like crocodiles. It shows how environmental factors, such as temperature, can play a significant role in shaping the development and characteristics of different species.

What is the origin of Ebola?

———

E bola is a virus that causes a severe and often deadly disease in humans and other primates.

The Ebola virus is believed to have originated in animals, particularly fruit bats. These bats are natural carriers of the virus, which means they can have the virus in their bodies without getting sick. It is thought that when humans come into contact with these infected bats or the bodily fluids of other animals that carry the virus, they can become infected with Ebola.

The exact way in which humans first came into contact with the Ebola virus is not entirely clear. However, it is believed that the transmission can occur through activities such as hunting, preparing or consuming infected animals, or coming into contact with their bodily fluids. In some cases, the virus can then spread from person to person through direct contact with infected bodily fluids, such as blood, vomit, or feces.

It's important to note that the Ebola virus does not typically spread easily like the common cold or flu. It requires close contact with infected individuals or their bodily fluids for the virus to be transmitted.

Scientists continue to study the origin and transmission of the Ebola virus to better understand how it spreads and how to prevent outbreaks in the future.

Are there any non-parasitic animals that have evolved from parasitic ancestors?

———

Yes, there are examples of non-parasitic animals that have evolved from parasitic ancestors.

In the animal kingdom, there are some cases where animals that were once parasites have evolved into non-parasitic forms. This means that they have changed over time and no longer rely on other organisms for their survival.

Evolution is a slow and gradual process that occurs over many generations. Sometimes, certain organisms start off as parasites, meaning they live on or inside another organism and depend on it for their survival. However, through changes in their environment or other factors, they may adapt and evolve into different lifestyles where they no longer need to be parasites.

One example of this is the ancestor of modern-day barnacles. Barnacles are marine animals that attach themselves to surfaces, such as rocks or the hulls of ships. They were once free-swimming organisms but have evolved to become sessile (stationary) and develop a protective shell. Although some species of barnacles are still parasitic, many have become non-parasitic over time.

Another example is the transition from parasitic lice to non-parasitic species. Lice are tiny insects that live on the bodies of mammals, including humans. However, certain species of lice have evolved to live in the feathers or fur of their hosts without causing harm. They have adapted to their environment and no longer rely on their hosts for survival.

These examples show that through the process of evolution, some animals have been able to break free from their parasitic lifestyles and develop new ways of living. It is important to note that not all parasites will evolve into non-parasitic forms, as it depends on various factors including their environment and available resources.

Can bird flu spread through eating infected chicken?

———

B ird flu is a type of influenza virus that primarily affects birds, especially poultry like chickens and ducks. While some strains of bird flu can infect humans, it is rare for the virus to spread from birds to humans through the consumption of properly cooked chicken meat or eggs.

The main concern with bird flu arises when there is direct contact with infected birds or their secretions, such as respiratory droplets or feces. People who work closely with infected birds, such as poultry farmers or veterinarians, are at higher risk of contracting the virus.

However, it's important to note that the transmission of bird flu from birds to humans is still relatively uncommon. Most cases of human infection occur through close and prolonged contact with infected birds, especially in settings where hygiene and safety precautions may be inadequate.

To prevent the spread of bird flu, it is important to follow proper food handling and cooking practices. Thoroughly cooking chicken meat and eggs can effectively kill the virus, making it safe for consumption.

Health authorities and organizations closely monitor outbreaks of bird flu to prevent its spread and protect public health. They provide guidelines and recommendations for handling poultry products safely and minimizing the risk of transmission.

Are there competing scientific theories to Darwin's Theory of Evolution?

———

No, there are no widely accepted scientific theories that compete with Darwin's Theory of Evolution.

Charles Darwin's Theory of Evolution is a well-established scientific theory that explains how species change over time through a process called natural selection. It has been supported by a large body of evidence and is widely accepted by the scientific community.

While there may be ongoing scientific debates and discussions about specific details and mechanisms within the theory, there is currently no alternative theory that provides a more comprehensive and widely accepted explanation for the diversity of life on Earth.

Scientists continue to study and explore different aspects of evolution to deepen our understanding of how species change and adapt. They may propose new ideas or hypotheses within the framework of Darwin's theory, but these are considered extensions or refinements rather than competing theories.

CHRISTOBAL WATSON HERNANDEZ

It is important to note that in science, theories are not simply opinions or guesses. They are well-supported explanations that have undergone rigorous testing and scrutiny. Darwin's Theory of Evolution has withstood extensive scientific investigation and remains the foundation of our understanding of how life has evolved on Earth.

Is there an animal with a brain but no heart?

––––––

O ne example of an animal with a brain but no heart is the flat-worm, also known as a planarian. Planarians are small, flat invertebrates that live in freshwater environments. They have a very simple circulatory system that does not include a heart.

Instead of a heart, planarians have a network of branching tubes called "tubules" that help transport oxygen and nutrients throughout their body. These tubules allow gases and nutrients to diffuse directly to their cells without the need for a central pumping organ like a heart.

Planarians are able to obtain oxygen through diffusion from the water they live in. Their flat shape helps to maximize the surface area for gas exchange, allowing oxygen to enter their body and carbon dioxide to leave.

Even without a heart, planarians are able to move and perform various activities using their brain and nervous system. Their brain helps them coordinate different functions and respond to their environment. They can sense light, detect food, and even regenerate their body parts if they get injured.

Do human-caused oceanic algal blooms have a measurable carbon capture effect?

———

Human-caused oceanic algal blooms, such as fertilizing the ocean with iron, do have the potential to capture carbon, but the extent of their carbon capture effect is still being studied.

Oceanic algal blooms occur when certain types of algae multiply rapidly in the ocean, forming large patches or blooms. These blooms can happen naturally, but scientists have also been studying ways to intentionally stimulate algal growth as a possible method to capture carbon dioxide from the atmosphere.

Algae are photosynthetic organisms that use sunlight and carbon dioxide to grow. During photosynthesis, they take in carbon dioxide and release oxygen, which helps to reduce the amount of carbon dioxide in the atmosphere.

When algal blooms occur, they can absorb significant amounts of carbon dioxide from the water, effectively capturing carbon. This is because the algae use the carbon dioxide dissolved in the water to grow and multiply. When the algae die and sink to the ocean floor, some of the carbon they have captured can be stored for long periods of time.

Scientists have been studying the potential of human-induced algal blooms as a method of carbon capture and storage. One approach involves adding nutrients, such as iron, to certain areas of the ocean to stimulate algal growth. However, the effectiveness of this method and its long-term impact on the environment are still subjects of ongoing research.

While algal blooms have the potential to capture carbon, it is important to consider the potential side effects and unintended consequences. Large-scale algal blooms can disrupt marine ecosystems, leading to changes in oxygen levels and affecting other marine organisms.

What makes bats a good disease vector?

━━━

Bats are considered good disease vectors because they possess certain characteristics and behaviors that contribute to their ability to carry and transmit diseases.

One reason is that bats have a unique immune system that allows them to carry viruses without getting sick themselves. This means they can be infected with a virus and still spread it to other animals or humans without showing any signs of illness.

Additionally, bats are skilled flyers, which enables them to cover long distances during their flights. This increases their chances of coming into contact with various species of animals, including humans. When bats interact with other animals or humans, there is a possibility of transferring diseases from one species to another.

Furthermore, bats often live in large colonies and roost together in caves, trees, or buildings. These close living quarters create opportunities for viruses to spread among bats. If a bat is carrying a virus, it can easily transmit it to other bats in the colony. In some cases, these viruses may have the potential to spill over to other animals or humans.

CHRISTOBAL WATSON HERNANDEZ

It is important to note that not all bats carry diseases, and the majority of bats do not pose a direct threat to humans. However, due to their unique characteristics and behaviors, bats have been associated with certain diseases and are considered important in the transmission of those diseases.

How do parrots pronounce sounds that are made with lips or teeth?

———

P arrots are fascinating creatures known for their ability to mimic human speech and other sounds. While they don't have lips or teeth like humans, they have developed some clever ways to produce sounds that involve lips or teeth.

Parrots do not have lips or teeth like humans, but they have a specialized vocal apparatus called the syrinx. The syrinx is located at the base of their trachea, where the windpipe splits into the bronchi (tubes that lead to the lungs). The syrinx is responsible for producing sounds in parrots.

When it comes to sounds made with lips, such as the "p" or "b" sounds, parrots can mimic these by using their beak and tongue. They position their beak in a certain way and use their tongue to create a similar sound effect. It may not be exactly the same as how humans produce these sounds, but parrots can make similar sounds that mimic lip movements.

As for sounds made with teeth, like the "th" sound, parrots again use their tongue and beak to create a similar effect. They position their tongue against their beak and use the airflow to produce a sound that is close to the "th" sound. While it may not be an exact replica of human pronunciation, parrots have the ability to imitate and approximate these sounds.

It's important to note that parrots have a remarkable ability to mimic sounds, but their vocal abilities may vary depending on the species and individual parrot. Some parrots are highly skilled at imitating a wide range of sounds, while others may have limitations in their vocal repertoire. Nonetheless, their adaptation of using the syrinx, beak, and tongue allows them to produce sounds that resemble those made with lips or teeth.

Are Bird courtship dances genetic or learned?

———

The courtship dances performed by birds can have both genetic and learned components.

Bird courtship dances involve specific movements and displays that birds perform to attract a mate. These dances can have a combination of genetic and learned elements.

First, let's talk about the genetic aspect. Some bird species have specific courtship behaviors and displays that are innate, meaning they are genetically programmed and passed down from parents to offspring. These innate behaviors are instinctual and do not require the bird to learn them. They are naturally expressed as part of the bird's courtship repertoire.

However, there is also a learned component to bird courtship dances. Birds can observe and learn courtship behaviors from other birds around them, including their parents or other members of their species. They may imitate the dances they see and incorporate them into their own courtship displays. This learning process allows birds to refine and adapt their courtship behaviors based on the social and environmental cues they encounter.

Will moist food spoil in low-pressure environments like a near-vacuum?

————

Moist food can spoil in low-pressure environments because of the conditions created by the lack of pressure. In a near-vacuum, the pressure is much lower than what we experience on Earth. This low pressure affects the boiling point of liquids, including the water content in food.

Normally, when we cook or heat food, the high temperature helps kill bacteria and other microorganisms that can cause spoilage. However, in a low-pressure environment, the boiling point of water decreases. This means that the water in moist food can start to boil even at lower temperatures, such as room temperature. As a result, the moisture in the food can evaporate more quickly, leading to dehydration and potential spoilage.

In addition, the low-pressure environment can also affect the growth of bacteria, yeast, and molds. Some microorganisms thrive in low-pressure environments and can multiply rapidly, leading to spoilage of the food. The absence of air pressure also affects the ability of certain microorganisms to survive or grow.

To prevent spoilage in low-pressure environments, it is important to properly store and package moist food to maintain its freshness. Vacuum-sealed packaging, for example, helps remove air and create a higher-pressure environment that slows down spoilage. Additionally, other preservation methods such as freezing or using preservatives can also help extend the shelf life of moist food.

Thank you for taking the time to read my book, if you enjoyed it please take a moment to leave a review on Amazon and Goodreads as that really helps me a lot.

If you would like to know when more books come out please follow me on FaceBook at: https://www.facebook.com/CristobalWatsonHernandez

Or scan the QR code below:

KNOWLEDGE DROPS - BIOLOGY 1

If you are an EFL teacher and would like to access lesson plans for the questions and answers in this book, please make sure to bookmark the google drive folder at:

https://drive.google.com/drive/folders/1I1AZuDRRYqDSuG-uXrsnIsMXQZzOP4On3?usp=sharing

Please keep an eye out for new lesson plans as they become available.

From the entire team at Chipped Feather Productions, we sincerely thank you for your support and patronage.

Also by Christobal Watson Hernandez

Knowledge Drops Biology
Knowledge Drops - Biology 1

www.ingramcontent.com/pod-product-compliance
Lightning Source LLC
Chambersburg PA
CBHW060947040426
42445CB00011B/1041